GDPR FOR HR PROFESSIONALS

BY DANIEL BARNETT

Published by Employment Law Services Limited, Unit 3, Chequers Farm, Chequers Lane, Watford, Hertfordshire WD25 0LG

ISBN 978-0-9553886-4-4

ACKNOWLEDGMENTS

Thank you first and foremost to Claire Scott for her help with researching the content and preparing a first draft of this book.

Thank you also to Christopher John Payne for his help with some of the technical stuff I needed to know for putting this book together, to Jennie Hargrove for her assistance getting it published, and to Jim Chute for his help with design and layout.

Finally, a big thank you to my family, Miranda, Tabby, Cressie and Rufus.

ABOUT THE AUTHOR

DANIEL BARNETT

Daniel Barnett is a leading employment law barrister practising from Outer Temple Chambers. With 25 years' experience defending public and private sector employers against employment claims, he has represented a Royal Family, several international airlines, FTSE-100 companies and various NHS Trusts and local authorities. Employee clients include David & Victoria Beckham's nanny and Paul Mason (subject of the ITV documentary 'Britain's Fattest Man').

Daniel is a past chair of the Employment Lawyers' Association's publishing committee and electronic services working party. He is the author or co-author of eight books, including the Law Society Handbook on Employment Law (currently in its 7th edition). He is the creator of the Employment Law (UK) mailing list, an email alerter bulletin service sending details of breaking news in employment law three times a week to 30,000 receipients.

Legal directories describe him as "extremely knowledgeable and [he] can absorb pages of instructions at lightning speed", "involved in a number of highly contentious matters", "singled out for his work for large blue-chip companies", "combination of in-depth legal knowledge, pragmatism, quick response times and approachability", "inexhaustible", "tenacious", "knowledgeable" and "an excellent advocate".

He Is one of the leading speakers and trainers on the employment law and HR circuit. He has presented seminars for the House of Commons, the BBC, Oxford University, HSBC, Barclays Bank, Ocado, and dozens of other organisations in-house. In 2013, 2014 and 2016 he designed and was the sole speaker at, the Employment Law MasterClass national tour. In 2016 and 2017 he presented the HR Secrets tour around the UK.

As well as full-time practice as a barrister and speaker, Daniel is an experienced entrepreneur. He is the founder and owner of Employment Law Services Ltd (a legal publishing company), which provides marketing and educational services to employment lawyers and HR professionals. In 2007, he co-founded CPD Webinars Ltd, then the UK's leading webinar training company for lawyers, and sold it to Thomson Reuters in 2011.

Daniel is widely sought after as a commentator in both broadcast and print media on all legal issues, and is the resident lawyer on LBC radio, where he co-presents the legal hour on Clive Bull's Wednesday evening show.

www.danielbarnett.co.uk

Outer Temple Chambers
Strand
London

March 2018

CONTENTS

Introduction

WHAT IS THE GDPR?

Data protection – it's not the sexiest topic. Many people have understandably had their heads in the sand for a while about the new regime. However, with only a few months to go and a draft Data Protection Bill winging its way through Parliament, it is time for us all to prepare for the new regime. I am going to keep this book as simple and practical as possible in what is a hugely detailed and complex area, spanning many different parts of the business, not just HR. But inevitably, we do need to delve into the principles a bit to understand the context for what you need to do next.

GDPR stands for a European regulation called the *General Data Protection Regulation*, which was formally adopted in April 2016 and comes into force across all EU Member States, including the UK, on 25 May this year.

The current data privacy rules in the UK come from the *Data Protection Act 1998*. But life has changed considerably since that legislation was introduced. It is now creaking under the weight of the modern world. Smartphones, tablets, social media, cloud computing, artificial intelligence, and the myriad of other technological advances in recent years, have meant the way in which we store and manage data has changed beyond recognition.

The GDPR is intended to provide a common set of rules across the EU that can meet the changing data protection landscape of the modern world and provide the right protection to individuals, or 'data subjects', as they are known.

HOW DOES IT AFFECT THE UK?

All businesses which have EU establishments that process personal data will have to comply with the GDPR. But it's broader than that. Even non-EU organisations will have to comply if they want to provide their goods or services to the EU or they want to monitor EU nationals.

The UK Government has introduced the Data Protection Bill, and when it comes into force, together with the GDPR, it will provide a modern data protection framework for the UK.

A quick word on Brexit at the start – when the UK leaves the EU, the GDPR will be copied and pasted into UK law (along with all other EU law) by the European Union (Withdrawal) Bill, which is also currently going through Parliament.

WHY SHOULD WE CARE?

The reason this has rocketed up board agendas is the consequences for businesses who do not comply.

Under the GDPR, fines will increase from the maximum fine of £500,000 under the 1998 Act (which was eye-watering enough) to the colossal €20 million (which is more than £17 million at the moment) or up to 4% of annual worldwide turnover (whichever is higher).

There are also various criminal offences in relation to any person who knowingly or recklessly obtains, discloses or retains personal data without the consent of the data controller (or employer). There are some limited defences. For example, if you can show that you had a reasonable belief that you either had consent or had a legal right to do so.

There has been a lot of press focus on data security breaches in recent years. So reputational damage is also a risk. TalkTalk, Yahoo, Sage and Morrisons supermarket are just some of those who have been all over the press as a result of data breaches.

Individuals will also be able to claim compensation for breach of the GDPR against data controllers and data processors. An employer may be both a data controller and a data processor. This compensation will cover financial loss etc., but also damages purely for distress.

There is no transition period for introduction of the GDPR. When the Data Protection Bill becomes law, it will apply immediately to all UK employers (and, of course, other businesses).

The Information Commissioner's Office has the regulatory powers in the UK. It will have wide-ranging powers to get information from employers, to require you to comply with the new regime and to issue penalties.

Before you panic though, it is expected that the ICO will continue to take a fairly sensible approach to enforcement. It might encourage organisations to take action to sort out a problem first. The most severe penalties are likely to be for significant breaches of obligation – in particular, in relation to data security.

HOW WILL IT AFFECT EMPLOYERS?

The new data protection rules will affect all areas of a business which process personal data, including data about customers, suppliers and website users. This is an issue for your entire business.

But clearly the data of employees, workers and consultants is also affected. In this book, I will refer to this group of data subjects collectively as 'employees', for ease, but the same rules apply in relation to workers and consultants etc. as well.

As employers, you process a lot of personal data on a day to day basis. This can be for various reasons, including:

- for background checks;
- for payroll and benefits admin;
- for insurance;
- for performance reviews, monitoring of employee activities, including attendance, dealing with disciplinaries and grievances;
- training; and
- for legal reasons.

The types of personal data processed are hugely wide ranging as well. Personal data could include:

- financial, personal and health information;
- emails, CCTV images, files notes, automated data, etc.

The personal data may not always be about the employee either. Take, for example, an email from your employee to her boss, which says, "I have to leave early tonight as my son has a doctor's appointment – he has a rash." Like this email, the personal data being used by employers may often include what has been known up until now as 'sensitive personal data', and which I will talk about some more later.

The introduction of GDPR in larger organisations is likely to be managed by legal or compliance teams, with input from IT, HR and many others. If you are in HR in a smaller organisation, however, it is much more likely to land firmly on your desk.

So, what do you need to know and what do you need to do?

Chapter 1

OVERVIEW OF IMPORTANT CONCEPTS AND PRINCIPLES

The approach of the GDPR (and therefore, the Data Protection Bill) is similar to the previous data protection laws, but it goes further. Employers, as data controllers, will still have to comply with a set of data protection principles for processing personal data. There is a new important principle of accountability, which requires employers to show that they have complied with these principles. And data subjects have a range of extended rights. These changes will involve a cultural shift by employers – putting data privacy and protection at the front and centre of their business.

Before we delve into the detail and look at the practical aspects of this for HR, it's important that we all understand a few key concepts and definitions under the GDPR and the DP Bill.

You will already be familiar with the concept of 'Personal Data'. It means information or data that relates to a living person who can be identified from that data. This includes information like names, addresses, contact details, employment details, financial information, disciplinary warnings, appraisals, or health records, for example.

It's important to note that personal data also includes any expression of opinion about that person and any indication of the intentions of the data controller or any other person in respect of that individual. For example, an email in which a manager says that she is considering performance management of an employee following a customer complaint.

We also know about 'Sensitive Personal Data'. This will now be referred to as a 'special category' of data and will have special rules for lawful processing, as you would expect. I will talk more about those special rules later. Sensitive personal data now includes data relating to:

- race or ethnic origin;
- religion, philosophical beliefs or political opinions;
- health;
- genetic or biometric data;
- sexual orientation or sex life; and
- trade union membership.

'Data Processing' is a wide definition and it applies to all kinds of processing of that data. So, it can include obtaining, recording or holding data. It can include carrying out any operation on the data – including organising, amending, retrieving, using, disclosing, deleting or destroying data.

DATA PROTECTION PRINCIPLES

The GDPR sets out various data protection principles, which employers must comply with when processing personal data. They are largely the same as the principles under the 1998 Act, with some differences. Broadly speaking, the principles are:

- personal data must be processed lawfully, fairly and in a transparent way.

- personal data must only be collected for specified legitimate purposes and processed for those purposes only.

- personal data must be limited to what is necessary for the purposes for which it is processed. This is a stricter requirement than under the 1998 Act.

- the personal data must be accurate and kept up to date. There is now a rule that inaccurate data must be removed quickly or corrected.

- personal data must not be kept for longer than necessary for its purpose.

- it should be processed securely and confidentially to ensure it is not lost, damaged or destroyed.

Employers now also have a duty to show compliance with these principles. It is not enough to say: "But we are not in breach of any of them". The best way of demonstrating compliance is likely to be more sophisticated data protection policies and beefed-up internal processes, including training. You must also retain records of processing activities. These records should include details of data retention periods, transfers of personal data outside of Europe, and details of the recipients of personal data. The ICO can request these records at any time.

Privacy is a cornerstone of the new regime. It should feed into everything businesses do, with the aim of a cultural shift.

As employers, you must now take steps to build privacy and data protection into your systems, subject to what is technically possible and the cost of it. Steps should be taken to minimise data collected and only use it for the specific purpose for which it was obtained. If you are thinking about a new HR or payroll system, for example, then data protection should be one of the things you consider when designing it. The hope is that data breaches will then become more unlikely.

Turning to how employers should process this personal data.

Employers need a lawful basis to process data. There are six potential lawful bases:

- the first lawful basis is if you have the consent of the employee (data subject). Consent is something that we are familiar with using for the processing of personal data for employees at the moment. However, this is not going to be as easy, going forward. I will talk more about relying on consent in chapter 2.

- the second lawful basis can be if it is necessary for the performance of a contract with the employee (such as the employment contract), or if it is necessary to take steps at the employee's request before entering into the contract (such as contacting an old employer for a reference, perhaps).

- the third lawful basis is if it is necessary for compliance with a legal obligation. This could be providing information to HMRC, or in relation to employment tribunal proceedings or court action.

- the fourth lawful basis is if it is necessary to protect the vital interests of the employee or someone else. This is thought to be if the person's life or health is in danger.

- the fifth lawful basis is if it is in the public interest (which seems less relevant in the employment context).

- the sixth lawful basis is if it is necessary for the purposes of the legitimate interests of the employer or a third party. However, this can be overridden by the interests and fundamental rights and freedoms of the employee.

I will talk about these in more detail and what they might mean for employers in chapter 3.

PROCESSING OF SENSITIVE PERSONAL DATA

You are only allowed to process sensitive personal data in specific situations. In addition to the rules that apply to personal data, you will only be able to process if:

- the employee has given their explicit consent; or

- the employee has clearly made the data public. For example, by posting it on Twitter; or

- to carry out rights and obligations under employment law. This is very helpful and could range from processing data to ensure the health and safety of workers, complying with discrimination and unfair dismissal laws, TUPE, etc.

- to establish, exercise or defend legal claims;

- to protect the vital interests of the employee or another person, where the employee is physically or legally incapable of giving consent; or

- for the assessment of the person's working capacity, either on the basis of UK law or in accordance with a contract with a health professional, such as an external occupational health provider.

(There are other public policy reasons you can process special categories of personal data, such as when it is necessary for reasons of substantial public interest, for the legitimate interests of a not-for-profit organisation, including a trade union, and processing personal data in relation to criminal convictions. I won't go into these in any more detail.)

A QUICK WORD ON TRANSFERS TO NON-EU COUNTRIES

Most of the law on this will stay the same as it is now. For example, transfers to countries that the European Commission has approved are OK (such as Canada and New Zealand). Otherwise, if you transfer data outside the EU, you can only do it if there are appropriate safeguards (defined in the GDPR) in place. For example, you must do it in line with a contract incorporating what is known as the 'EU model clauses'. There are a couple of new methods of transfer incorporated into the GDPR too, but I won't go into these.

Chapter 2

CONSENT – AND THE PROBLEM WITH RELYING ON IT

So what is the deal with consent now?

Getting the consent of the employee to processing their personal data was usually the option we all took under the old 1998 Act. We are all used to putting a data protection clause in the contract of employment, which was then relied upon to prove the employee had given consent. This might have gone alongside a data protection policy and other notices. Consent would be implied unless there was an objection. Not so now.

The ICO hasn't really liked employers relying on consent to process personal data for a while now. This is because of the way the employment relationship works – employers usually hold all the cards. The balance of power lies with them. An employee doesn't really have much option but to accept the clause as it is part of the contract. Most employers are unlikely to negotiate on this clause, and the employee would have no real choice but to accept it or walk away from the job. This imbalance of power can also be seen when the employee is working in the role. At that stage, it is usually even more difficult for an employee to refuse to give consent to something like this – particularly if it is presented by the employer as a completely normal and standard term.

To rely on consent now, it must be:

- freely given;
- specific;
- informed; and
- unambiguous.

Also, if you are processing a special category of personal data (i.e. sensitive personal data) then, as I mentioned earlier, the consent must be explicit.

We can't just stick a consent clause in the employment contract and assume consent has been given. Even if contracts are not issued on a 'take it or leave it' basis, the employee may still feel under pressure to accept the clause or lose the job, or suffer some other form of detriment. If there is no genuine choice then consent cannot be freely given.

Consent needs to be 'distinguishable' – this means that it should be separate from other things. It can't be buried in amongst other policies or the employment contract. There should be a separate signature box from other parts of a document to make it clear the employee is giving consent to the data processing.

Occasionally, an employer may meet these requirements for consent though. For example, if you get specific consent to the sharing of personal data with an external occupational health consultant or to confirm the details of someone's salary to their mortgage provider. This sort of consent is specifically for those purposes and covers specific data. The consent is likely to be given at that time (as it will be in the person's interest to give it). However, it is unlikely to always be as easy as this.

A wide blanket consent won't be specific enough now. You have to list each purpose separately – for example, you have to say, "We intend to process your personal data for payroll and for monitoring your activities." Each would have to be set out separately and you would need to allow the employee to consent (or not) to each one. Arguably, you may be able to lump certain purposes together, but there is always a risk that this is then challenged for not being specific or clear enough.

There are also some practical problems for employers if you rely on consent:

- you might have to stop processing and seek consent (or rely on a new lawful ground) each time you need to process a different category of personal data from the original consent – this would obviously be unworkable.

- there is the problem if consent is not given – either because the employee ignores the request or doesn't want to consent for some reason.

- finally, the employee can withdraw consent at any time and the employer must tell the employee of this right. It should be as easy to withdraw consent as it is to give it. The employee should be able to withdraw consent to any of the types of processing, while still consenting to the others if he/she wants to. You should tell the employee how he or she can withdraw the consent and make it as easy as possible to do that. For example, fill in this form, email this person, press this button.

The onus is on you to show that the employee gave lawful consent, and you should keep appropriate records.

So we have established that most of the time, consent is not going to be an appropriate ground for you to rely on now when processing employees' personal data. I think that it should really be a last resort.

And if consent is not going to help employers, what is? Well don't worry – you can consider one of the other lawful grounds instead.

Chapter 3

OTHER LAWFUL BASES FOR PROCESSING DATA

As well as consent, there are other lawful grounds for processing under the GDPR.

IS IT NECESSARY FOR THE PERFORMANCE OF THE EMPLOYMENT CONTRACT (OR ANY OTHER CONTRACT TO WHICH THE EMPLOYEE IS PARTY)?

This will be a very helpful ground for employers, although we don't yet know how 'necessary' the data should be. Taking a really obvious example, you will definitely be able to use this ground to justify holding an employee's personal data to process their salary or other benefits. This is because pay is integral to the performance of the contract – the employee won't carry out work without pay. And it is necessary to process the hours worked and the amount of wages to be able to pay the employee.

However, will this ground be wide enough to justify holding other personal data that helps you as an employer? For example, what happens if you are holding or using personal data in case you need to use it for a disciplinary investigation? Is that necessary for the performance of the employment contract? You may think it is, but the employee may disagree. Even more tenuous will be where you are processing data to improve the performance of the business in some way. It could be because you are thinking about a restructure or a merger. It could be in relation to some form of marketing or business development. It could be to assist another area of the business or another group of employees. It becomes less and less likely that these sorts of reasons would come under the banner of 'necessary for the performance of the employment contract'.

Let's see if there are other grounds that could help instead.

COMPLIANCE WITH A LEGAL OBLIGATION

This will certainly be helpful when you have to disclose information to HMRC for tax purposes, or if you work in a regulated sector. You will also be able to rely on it to comply with a disclosure request from a tribunal or court. However, I don't think that this will cover most personal data processing that you need to do.

PROTECTING THE EMPLOYEE'S VITAL INTERESTS

Well, you might be able to rely upon this where you are holding and processing information about the employee's emergency contacts or to hold a record of an employee's allergies. But this won't help in most situations.

I think the most helpful category for employers is actually going to be:

PROCESSING PERSONAL DATA IN PURSUIT OF THE EMPLOYER'S 'LEGITIMATE INTERESTS'.

It will be important to use the other categories first, if you can, as this one is more open to challenge, but this is likely to be the most helpful category for employers.

It is lawful to process personal data that is necessary to achieve your 'legitimate interests', unless those interests are overridden by the interests or fundamental rights and freedoms of the employees.

There are special rules for public authorities.

Essentially, it's a balancing exercise. And it's for the employer to establish that they have compelling enough grounds to continue processing the data. The ICO confirms that the legitimate interests can be your own interests or those of a third party. They can include commercial or individual interests, or 'broader societal benefits'.

The processing must be necessary. If you can reasonably achieve the same result in another less intrusive way, legitimate interests will not apply.

You must balance your interests against the employee's. If the employee would not reasonably expect the processing or if it would cause unjustified harm, their interests are likely to override yours.

There is another important point here. If you intend to rely on the 'legitimate interests' ground then you must tell the employees which specific interests are being pursued. You might say: "To run your business profitably or to comply with a customer contract."

You have to notify them of this because data subjects have a right to object to how you handle their information for a specific purpose. If they object, and you haven't got a policy/privacy notice that demonstrates that you had told them of the specific legitimate interest you were relying on, then you will have an uphill struggle to prove that your interests override theirs. If you can't show this then you have to stop the processing. I will consider the notification requirements in chapter 4.

Chapter 4

INFORMATION TO BE GIVEN TO EMPLOYEES

PROVIDING INFORMATION ON DATA

You will be aware that under the 1998 Act, employers had to give job applicants and employees a privacy of 'fair processing' notice, which set out the purposes for which data is processed, along with any other information needed to ensure fair processing of that data.

Under the new rules, employers must still do this, but also must provide information on the legal basis for processing. All information must be concise, transparent, easily accessible, and given in plain language.

In the employment context, this sort of information is most likely to be provided in a data protection policy or other privacy notice and the contract of employment. However, a privacy notice could also be worked into a job application pack, training materials, website notices, and so on.

You must tell the employee:

- the identity of the data controller (employer) and any data protection officer.

- the purpose of the processing and the lawful basis you are relying on.

- if you are relying on a legitimate interest, as I mentioned, you need to specify that interest.

- the source and category of the data (unless it has come from the employee themselves).

- who will receive the personal data? This doesn't need to be the names of people. It is enough to say the categories of people who will receive it, for example, the payroll department or the company's occupational health provider.

- the period the data will be stored for. If that's not possible though, then you need to tell the employee the criteria that you will use to work out the period. For example, during the person's employment and for three years following termination of employment.

- you need to tell the employees of their data subject rights. I will talk about these in more detail in chapter 5.

- as I have already mentioned, you must also tell the employee that they have the right to withdraw consent, if consent is being relied upon as a legal basis for processing.

- you must also highlight the right of the employee to complain to the ICO.

- if the data is going to be transferred to a country outside the EU then you must also tell the employee the legal basis for this transfer and the safeguards in place.

- you must also tell them about any automated decision making or profiling.

The information that needs to be provided is a lot more than you have to give at the moment.

HOW AND WHEN TO PROVIDE THE DETAIL

Your policy or notice needs to be concise, accessible and in plain language. The information should be given at the time the data is obtained from the employee or within a reasonable period if it is obtained from someone else. The ICO suggests within one month of processing.

AN EVIDENCE TRAIL

Make sure that you keep a record of the information given and the people who have received it. You could do this by asking employees to sign and return or otherwise acknowledge the policy. The main thing is that you can show you have complied with your legal obligations if you ever need to.

DATA PROTECTION OFFICERS

Public authorities and employers whose core activities involve systematic monitoring or large-scale processing of sensitive personal data must have a Data Protection Officer. For example, if you monitor the behaviour of data subjects online as part of your business then you would need one.

Employers in the financial services, insurance or other regulated industries are likely to be affected more here. Just because you process sensitive personal data as an employer, doesn't mean that you need a DPO though. You are unlikely to be processing it on such a large-scale that you need to appoint a DPO. It is likely to be for employers whose core business involves this sort of large-scale processing instead.

Although this won't apply to all employers, some will also want to appoint a DPO voluntarily (or a Data Protection Manager). I know that some of you will have already done this.

If you do appoint a DPO then their main role is to keep you on the right side of your legal obligations and be responsible for compliance. The GDPR has specific rules for the DPOs, and there are helpful EU Guidelines on DPOs if you need to look at them.

DATA PROTECTION IMPACT ASSESSMENTS

I also want to say a quick word about 'Data Protection Impact Assessments'. If you are in a larger organisation, you may be familiar with these already. They are to help you identify the most effective way to comply with your data protection obligations. The ICO recommends using them, and has a good code of practice that sets out how to conduct them in a lot more detail.

You only have to do an impact assessment under the GDPR where you are processing in a way that is likely to result in a high risk to the rights and freedoms of individuals. This is particularly the case when using new technology.

Whether what you are doing is high risk will be fact specific, but could include:

- if you are processing in a systematic and extensive way. This could be doing automated processing or profiling, which has legal or other significant effects on individuals. I imagine the insurance and consumer industries will be caught by this, but there will be others.

- analysing or predicting aspects of performance at work, finances, health, personal preferences or interests, reliability or behaviour, location or movements, or to create or use personal profiles.

- large scale or systematic monitoring of data in relation to criminal convictions or CCTV in public areas. Clearly, this affects government and the public sector more.

However, if you are a private sector employer who uses technology and automation to process large amounts of personal data then this could apply to you.

In assessing whether something you are doing is high risk, you may wish to take a look at the EU guidelines to help you. (Guidelines on Data Protection Impact Assessment and determining whether processing is 'likely to result in a high risk' for the purposes of Regulation 2016/679.)

BREACHES OF SECURITY

We are all aware of examples of breaches of data security. Whether it is sending an email to the wrong person, losing a memory stick, or leaving a laptop on a train. It can happen accidentally (and far less common deliberately – such as in the case of Morrisons supermarket, where an employee held a grudge and uploaded 100,000 of his colleagues' personal data to the internet).

Under the new GDPR rules, if there is a personal data breach that is likely to result in a 'risk to the rights and freedoms of individuals' then employers must notify the ICO promptly and within 72 hours if possible. If the report is made outside this timeframe, you must provide a 'reasoned justification' for the delay. You don't need to notify the ICO if there is no risk to data subjects, because, for example, the data was encrypted. An example of a risk to data subjects would be if they were laid open to the risk of identity theft.

If you are notifying the ICO of a breach, you must tell them what happened and how many people roughly are likely to be affected. You must also inform the ICO of the likely consequences and the measures you are taking or planning to take. You must tell any data subject whose data security is at high risk following the breach.

You must keep a record of all data breaches and the action you have taken – even if there was no obligation to tell the ICO because the data was encrypted.

I recommend that you introduce clear internal processes so that everyone is clear in which situations a breach needs to be notified and who has responsibility for making those decisions. A three-day time limit is extremely tight, so it's important that people understand the urgency of reporting a breach and who to tell. That person or team should also have training on how to assess whether a breach needs to be reported and what measures should be taken following a breach. Much of this comes back to the cultural shift that the GDPR intends to create – putting data security at the front and centre of your business.

DANIEL
BARNETT

Chapter 5

THE RIGHTS OF EMPLOYEES AS DATA SUBJECTS

What are the employees' rights under GDPR?

Employees have a new package of rights. They have the right to:

- information (as I covered in chapter 4);

- access their own personal data;

- correct personal data;

- erase personal data (the right to be forgotten);

- restrict data processing;

- object to data processing;

- receive a copy of their personal data or transfer their personal data to another data controller;

- not be subject to automated decision-making (with some exceptions); and

- be notified of a data security breach.

The ICO has more information on these rights.

I will firstly deal with accessing personal data – or as we know them:

SUBJECT ACCESS REQUESTS

The SARs right is pretty similar to the existing rules under the 1998 Act. In addition, the employer now needs to provide information in relation to:

- the planned period for storage of data;

- details of the employees' rights (to rectify or erase data and rights to restrict or object to the processing and to complain to the ICO); and

- the safeguards applied on a transfer of data outside the EU.

The ICO website has full details.

As you know, at the moment, an employer has 40 days to comply with a SAR. This period will go. You will now have to comply without undue delay and within one month. It's important that you update your internal processes to meet this tighter time requirement. You may want to prepare template letters and give the relevant employees training.

There is an ability to get an extension of an additional two months if necessary, if the requests are complex or numerous.

The £10 fee to make a subject access request is being abolished. However, if a request is 'manifestly unfounded or excessive', you can charge a 'reasonable' fee, taking into account administrative costs.

You may also refuse to act on the request altogether in these circumstances. When doing so, you must tell the employee of their right to complain to the ICO.

Before you think that this is your get out of jail free card – a word of warning. Just because you think the request is unfounded or excessive, doesn't mean the ICO will agree. The ICO has already indicated that these provisions will only apply in the most extreme cases and can't be used to evade your obligations. The Explanatory notes in the DP Bill give an example of a 'manifestly unfounded and excessive request' as one that repeats the substance of previous requests.

The Data Protection Bill keeps various legal exemptions so that you wouldn't need to respond to a SAR in particular situations. For example, if the personal data being requested is legally privileged.

It will also be a criminal offence under the new legislation to change or conceal information instead of responding to a SAR.

THE RIGHT TO BE FORGOTTEN

The next right I wanted to mention is the right to be forgotten (also referred to as the right to 'erasure' (and no, not the 80s pop duo). The right to be forgotten can be exercised by the employee if:

- the data processing is no longer necessary for the purposes for which it was collected or processed.

- the data has been unlawfully processed (for example, you have relied on consent that has not met the conditions I mentioned in chapter 2, or you have sent a defective privacy notice that has not set out the correct information, as I talked about in chapter 4);

- the processing is based on the 'legitimate interest' condition and the employee objects and you cannot prove you have 'overriding legitimate grounds' for continuing.

You may have to update your IT systems to ensure that you can delete the personal data from your systems completely if required. You will also have to make sure that the relevant staff know what they have to do in these circumstances.

THE RIGHT TO RESTRICT PROCESSING

The employee has a right to block or restrict the processing of his or her personal data in a variety of situations, including:

- where the processing is unlawful;

- where he/she contests the data's accuracy;

- where you rely upon the 'legitimate interest' basis for processing and the employee objects and says that his or her rights override yours. I can see this being used by employees facing disciplinary proceedings – particularly if you have carried out a covert investigation. The employee may argue that his/her right to privacy trumps your legitimate interests.

When processing is restricted, you are allowed to store the personal data, but not to process it any further than that. The ICO website has more on this. Again, you will have to ensure that the relevant staff know about the changes and that your systems have the capability to restrict this data.

THE RIGHT TO RECTIFICATION

The employee has the right to request that data that is inaccurate or incomplete is corrected (or rectified).

You usually have to comply with any such request within one month. If you have disclosed the personal data to third parties, you must inform them of the correction. You must also tell the employee to which third parties you disclosed the incorrect data.

DATA PORTABILITY

Employees can ask you to share their personal data with a third party. This should be done without a financial charge or undue delay. It should also usually be done within one month.

Chapter 6

TEN PRACTICAL STEPS TO PREPARE FOR THE GDPR

If you are feeling overwhelmed, you are most definitely not the only one. However, there are plenty of practical steps you can take now to be ready for the new data protection regime.

STEP 1 – RAISE AWARENESS AND GET BUY-IN FROM THE TOP.

The new data protection compliance regime is not just an HR issue. It affects the whole business, and the potential sanctions are so eye-watering that if they aren't already, the directors and top management should be sitting up and taking notice.

This planning takes time and costs money. The effort to get ready needs buy-in from the top to ensure you have the resources available to be on track for when the new law comes into force. It's important to understand who is responsible for delivering GDPR compliance in your business. As I have already said, in larger businesses, this might fall to compliance or legal to run with input from commercial. However, in smaller organisations, a director may be responsible and rely heavily on HR to implement. As HR professionals, you need to know what you are expected to do, and obviously bring in expertise (such as assistance from IT and managers on the ground) as necessary to complete the project.

If you are behind in your planning, don't worry. Keep going! The ICO are likely to be a lot tougher on businesses that have done nothing to get ready for GDPR than those who have, even if you need to refine those plans after the GDPR is in force.

STEP 2 – DO A DATA AUDIT.

You need to work out what personal data you currently control and/or process and where exactly that data goes and what is done with it.

How is it collected? Is it on an application form, is it collated from managers or from the employee themselves? What happens to the information after you have collected it? Is it disposed of after a decision has been made or is it held in your systems or in the employee's file? How secure is that data? Would you be able to detect a security breach? How and when is data disposed of?

This is all likely to involve some investigation and communication with other parts of the business and even external providers. You may need IT and management assistance for this.

STEP 3 – ANALYSE THE REASONS THAT PARTICULAR DATA IS OBTAINED CURRENTLY.

For example, do you currently collect and hold data for payroll purposes? Is it held for emergencies? Or for carrying out your contracts or in case of legal action? Is the data actually used or does it just stay somewhere, metaphorically (or literally) gathering dust?

Let's take the example of sickness records. In HR, you will have a record of how often an employee is absent on sick leave. This is perfectly legitimate for various reasons – you might be keeping the data to ensure that you pay sick pay in accordance with the law and the contract. You may be monitoring whether or not the employee is hitting unacceptable sickness levels, which might need management. But how long do you keep that data for? Do you have a system for deleting the data at the end of a year (assuming that this fits with your policies on sickness absence?) Or does it just sit on the employee's file? Does the reason you hold that data change if you have been notified of an employee's disability? You might be holding it to ensure you comply with your legal duty to make reasonable adjustments. The parameters in which you judge unacceptable absence are likely to change for someone with a disability. Does that affect why or how long you hold on to the data?

You should go through this thought process for each category of data.

Have you just relied on a blanket consent hidden somewhere in the contract of employment (or other document) to allow you to do whatever you like with an employee's data (or the data of a worker, consultant, trainee, apprentice, or job applicant)? Is the original reason you collected or used the data still relevant?

STEP 4 – CONSIDER WHICH LEGAL BASIS YOU WILL RELY ON GOING FORWARD FOR PROCESSING, AND REMEMBER THE DATA PROTECTION PRINCIPLES.

Which of the reasons set out in chapter 3 will you rely on to process the data now? You are unlikely to be able to rely on consent now for most things. So which will you choose? Remember, the grounds are:

- consent of the data subject;

- necessary for the performance of a contract with the data subject;

- necessary for compliance with a legal obligation;

- necessary to protect vital interests of a data subject or someone else;

- if it is in the public's interest; or

- if it is necessary for the purposes of legitimate interests.

Think about the data protection principles I covered at the start of chapter 1. Consider whether you need to make changes to which personal data you process and how you do it, to stay in line with these principles. For example:

- consider processing personal data in a way so that you can't tell from looking at it which person it relates to. You would need additional information (a key or code) kept separately (and securely) to decode it. (Known as 'pseudonymisation'.)

- think about whether some data can be anonymised. Do you really need to be able to identify the employee to use the data? For example, if you are processing information for research or statistics then you could probably anonymise it. We see this a lot in the public sector when data is collated for the purposes of equal opportunities.

- use passwords and encourage employees to use more complex passwords, not to share them, and to change them regularly.

- encrypt data where possible, particularly if you are transferring data or allowing remote working.

- think about the devices that employees use and their security access. Will you still allow employees to use their own smartphones etc., or will you provide company phones and laptops now instead?

- only process personal data necessary for specific purposes.

- put in place measures to ensure you are compliant with the principles.

- keep records to prove you are compliant.

STEP 5 – REVIEW AND UPDATE YOUR EMPLOYMENT CONTRACTS AND POLICIES.

As I have already discussed, standard blanket consents in an employment contract will not work and the easiest thing is probably just to remove them. This will be easy enough for new staff. However, remember for existing staff that you may need to consider a process for changing terms and conditions, or at the very least, informing them that the employer will no longer be relying upon the consent in their contract, and instead, will be relying on one of the other grounds, which you should specify.

You will need to update staff handbooks and put in place some new policies too. These policies will need to guide staff in how to comply with GDPR. They will also form important evidence of your compliance. The main one to focus on first is the data protection policy (and any other privacy notices you have). These will need to be rewritten to take account of all the new principles and concepts I have already talked about. You may be able to combine these. It doesn't matter what you call them, as long as they set out all the relevant information.

Depending upon your business, you may also wish to introduce policies on data retention and destruction, record-keeping, data security, and how to deal with subject access requests.

You also need to look at your other policies to see whether the new data protection regime will have an effect on them. The most obvious of these is the disciplinary and grievance procedures. It's important to make sure that any data breaches will be a disciplinary offence. If you allow home or remote working then you should update that policy to take account of data security and protection. For example, requiring encryption of data or banning the use of memory sticks out of the office. If you have policies in relation to monitoring IT, personal devices etc. then they should also be checked.

STEP 6 – CHECK AND UPDATE YOUR INTERNAL PROCESSES.

Someone in the business needs to make sure that all of the necessary processes are in place in relation to how you collect and use data, and who is responsible for each stage, so that the business complies with the new regime.

If that person is you, you should familiarise yourself with the relevant ICO guidance as a minimum.

You should have processes to ensure that employees can use their new rights easily. For example, what will you do if someone objects to the use of their personal data for something, or asks for it to be restricted or corrected?

You should also introduce clear processes for the detection of security breaches and for what happens if there is a breach including how and when it needs to be reported to the ICO.

STEP 7 – REVIEW AND UPDATE YOUR EXTERNAL CONTRACTS AND PROCESSES.

Where you share personal data with third party service providers, the business should ensure that any contracts with these 'data processors' set out clearly the data protection obligations and the contractual consequences of any breach. This could include contracts with IT cloud providers, benefit providers, payroll departments, OH providers and so on. This is unlikely to fall to HR, but it's important that it is on someone's list!

Internal processes should also be clear so that third parties are told of changes to personal data as necessary.

You should also make sure that the business is ready to deal with requests from employees to share their data with third parties. For example, an employee's personal data should be easily identified and turned into a format that can quickly be sent to the third party in an easy to read format. You may already have this sort of system in place, but if not, you are likely to need some IT input here.

STEP 8 – IDENTIFY WHO IS RESPONSIBLE FOR DATA PROTECTION COMPLIANCE IN YOUR BUSINESS.

Do you need to recruit? Do you require the appointment of a Data Protection Officer?

If you are not one of the employers who must have a DPO, do you want one anyway? You may at least want a dedicated Data Protection Manager (or team) who deals with data protection for you. If budget is a problem, can you make use of a consultant until you get used to the new regime?

STEP 9 – TRAINING.

Make sure that those who are going to be responsible for compliance with the GDPR going forward have adequate training, resources and help so that they don't feel under undue pressure. Otherwise, in addition to non-compliance, the business may face sickness absences and employment tribunal claims.

STEP 10 – KEEP COMPLIANT!

It's really important that you keep your policies and processes under review to ensure that the business remains compliant in the future. I would suggest an annual audit of how data is processed and regular training as new employees join or change roles. Your Data Protection Officer or Manager may wish to start doing spot checks from time to time, particularly in higher risk areas.

Remind your staff that if the reason for processing data changes in respect of an employee (or group of employees) then employees should be informed of that, in accordance with the rules we have talked about today.

Some larger employers may want to introduce an annual form for managers to sign perhaps at appraisal time (or, for example, an online tick box) to say that they understand and have complied with the data protection policies. Any changes should also be reflected in your policies and notices.

I suggest that those responsible for data protection keep up to date with the ICO guidance and codes of practice as they develop.

Chapter 7

CONCLUSION

Here are some key messages to take away on the new data protection regime and what you as an HR professional should be doing now:

1. encourage a culture shift from the top-down, putting data protection front and centre;

2. do a data audit and work out what will be your legal bases for data processing;

3. review your contracts, policies and processes, and update them as necessary;

4. encourage regular reviews and training of key personnel on GDPR;

5. and finally, above all – keep calm and carry on! You will already be doing an awful lot of good stuff as a business (and particularly in the HR team) in the area of data protection.

Your old ways of working and policies and procedures will certainly need to be reviewed, and some changes and updates may be needed. But hopefully, this will be more in the area of sensible tweaks and a few new policies and processes, rather than a fundamental change to the way your business operates.

APPENDIX A

PREPARING FOR THE GENERAL DATA PROTECTION REGULATION

Published by the Information Commissioner's Office, licensed under the Open Government licence.

Preparing for the General Data Protection Regulation (GDPR)

12 steps to take now

Published by the Information Commissioner's Office, licensed under the Open Government licence.

1

Awareness

You should make sure that decision makers and key people in your organisation are aware that the law is changing to the GDPR. They need to appreciate the impact this is likely to have.

2

Information you hold

You should document what personal data you hold, where it came from and who you share it with. You may need to organise an information audit.

3

Communicating privacy information

You should review your current privacy notices and put a plan in place for making any necessary changes in time for GDPR implementation.

4

Individuals' rights

You should check your procedures to ensure they cover all the rights individuals have, including how you would delete personal data or provide data electronically and in a commonly used format.

5

Subject access requests

You should update your procedures and plan how you will handle requests within the new timescales and provide any additional information.

6

Lawful basis for processing personal data

You should identify the lawful basis for your processing activity in the GDPR, document it and update your privacy notice to explain it.

V2.0 201705

7 Consent

You should review how you seek, record and manage consent and whether you need to make any changes. Refresh existing consents now if they don't meet the GDPR standard.

8 Children

You should start thinking now about whether you need to put systems in place to verify individuals' ages and to obtain parental or guardian consent for any data processing activity.

9 Data breaches

You should make sure you have the right procedures in place to detect, report and investigate a personal data breach.

10 Data Protection by Design and Data Protection Impact Assessments

You should familiarise yourself now with the ICO's code of practice on Privacy Impact Assessments as well as the latest guidance from the Article 29 Working Party, and work out how and when to implement them in your organisation.

11 Data Protection Officers

You should designate someone to take responsibility for data protection compliance and assess where this role will sit within your organisation's structure and governance arrangements. You should consider whether you are required to formally designate a Data Protection Officer.

12 International

If your organisation operates in more than one EU member state (ie you carry out cross-border processing), you should determine your lead data protection supervisory authority. Article 29 Working Party guidelines will help you do this.

ico.org.uk

Information Commissioner's Office

INTRODUCTION

Many of the GDPR's main concepts and principles are much the same as those in the current Data Protection Act (DPA), so if you are complying properly with the current law then most of your approach to compliance will remain valid under the GDPR and can be the starting point to build from. However, there are new elements and significant enhancements, so you will have to do some things for the first time and some things differently.

It is important to use this checklist and other Information Commissioner's Office (ICO) resources to work out the main differences between the current law and the GDPR. The ICO is producing new guidance and other tools to assist you, as well as contributing to guidance that the Article 29 Working Party is producing at the European level. These are all available via the ICO's Overview of the General Data Protection Regulation. The ICO is also working closely with trade associations and bodies representing the various sectors – you should also work closely with these bodies to share knowledge about implementation in your sector.

It is essential to plan your approach to GDPR compliance now and to gain 'buy in' from key people in your organisation. You may need, for example, to put new procedures in place to deal with the GDPR's new transparency and individuals' rights provisions. In a large or complex business this could have significant budgetary, IT, personnel, governance and communications implications.

The GDPR places greater emphasis on the documentation that data controllers must keep to demonstrate their accountability. Compliance with all the areas listed in this document will require organisations to review their approach to governance and how they manage data protection as a corporate issue. One aspect of this might be to review the contracts and other arrangements you have in place when sharing data with other organisations.

Some parts of the GDPR will have more of an impact on some organisations than on others (for example, the provisions relating to

profiling or children's data), so it would be useful to map out which parts of the GDPR will have the greatest impact on your business model and give those areas due prominence in your planning process.

AWARENESS

You should make sure that decision makers and key people in your organisation are aware that the law is changing to the GDPR. They need to appreciate the impact this is likely to have and identify areas that could cause compliance problems under the GDPR. It would be useful to start by looking at your organisation's risk register, if you have one.

Implementing the GDPR could have significant resource implications, especially for larger and more complex organisations. You may find compliance difficult if you leave your preparations until the last minute.

INFORMATION YOU HOLD

You should document what personal data you hold, where it came from and who you share it with. You may need to organise an information audit across the organisation or within particular business areas.

The GDPR requires you to maintain records of your processing activities. It updates rights for a networked world. For example, if you have inaccurate personal data and have shared this with another organisation, you will have to tell the other organisation about the inaccuracy so it can correct its own records. You won't be able to do this unless you know what personal data you hold, where it came from and who you share it with. You should document this. Doing this will also help you to comply with the GDPR's accountability principle, which requires organisations to be able to show how they comply with the data protection principles, for example by having effective policies and procedures in place.

COMMUNICATING PRIVACY INFORMATION

You should review your current privacy notices and put a plan in place for making any necessary changes in time for GDPR implementation.

When you collect personal data you currently have to give people certain information, such as your identity and how you intend to use their information. This is usually done through a privacy notice. Under the GDPR there are some additional things you will have to tell people. For example, you will need to explain your lawful basis for processing the data, your data retention periods and that individuals have a right to complain to the ICO if they think there is a problem with the way you are handling their data. The GDPR requires the information to be provided in concise, easy to understand and clear language.

The ICO's Privacy notices code of practice reflects the new requirements of the GDPR.

INDIVIDUALS' RIGHTS

You should check your procedures to ensure they cover all the rights individuals have, including how you would delete personal data or provide data electronically and in a commonly used format.

The GDPR includes the following rights for individuals:

- the right to be informed;

- the right of access;

- the right to rectification;

- the right to erasure;

- the right to restrict processing;

- the right to data portability;

- the right to object; and

- the right not to be subject to automated decision-making including profiling.

On the whole, the rights individuals will enjoy under the GDPR are the same as those under the DPA but with some significant enhancements. If you are geared up to give individuals their rights now, then the transition to the GDPR should be relatively easy. This is a good time to check your procedures and to work out how you would react if someone asks to have their personal data deleted, for example. Would your systems help you to locate and delete the data? Who will make the decisions about deletion?

The right to data portability is new. It only applies:

- to personal data an individual has provided to a controller;

- where the processing is based on the individual's consent or for the performance of a contract; and

- when processing is carried out by automated means.

You should consider whether you need to revise your procedures and make any changes. You will need to provide the personal data in a structured commonly used and machine readable form and provide the information free of charge.

SUBJECT ACCESS REQUESTS

You should update your procedures and plan how you will handle requests to take account of the new rules:

- in most cases you will not be able to charge for complying with a request.

- you will have a month to comply, rather than the current 40 days.

- you can refuse or charge for requests that are manifestly unfounded or excessive.

- if you refuse a request, you must tell the individual why and that they have the right to complain to the supervisory authority and to a judicial remedy. You must do this without undue delay and at the latest, within one month.

If your organisation handles a large number of access requests, consider the logistical implications of having to deal with requests more quickly.

You could consider whether it is feasible or desirable to develop systems that allow individuals to access their information easily online.

Lawful basis for processing personal data

You should identify the lawful basis for your processing activity in the GDPR, document it and update your privacy notice to explain it.

Many organisations will not have thought about their lawful basis for processing personal data. Under the current law this does not have many practical implications. However, this will be different under the GDPR

because some individuals' rights will be modified depending on your lawful basis for processing their personal data. The most obvious example is that people will have a stronger right to have their data deleted where you use consent as your lawful basis for processing.

You will also have to explain your lawful basis for processing personal data in your privacy notice and when you answer a subject access request. The lawful bases in the GDPR are broadly the same as the conditions for processing in the DPA. It should be possible to review the types of processing activities you carry out and to identify your lawful basis for doing so. You should document your lawful bases in order to help you comply with the GDPR's 'accountability' requirements.

CONSENT

You should review how you seek, record and manage consent and whether you need to make any changes. Refresh existing consents now if they don't meet the GDPR standard.

You should read the detailed guidance the ICO has published on consent under the GDPR, and use our consent checklist to review your practices. Consent must be freely given, specific, informed and unambiguous. There must be a positive opt-in – consent cannot be inferred from silence, pre- ticked boxes or inactivity. It must also be separate from other terms and conditions, and you will need to have simple ways for people to withdraw consent. Public authorities and employers will need to take particular care. Consent has to be verifiable and individuals generally have more rights where you rely on consent to process their data.

You are not required to automatically 'repaper' or refresh all existing DPA consents in preparation for the GDPR. But if you rely on individuals' consent to process their data, make sure it will meet the GDPR standard on being specific, granular, clear, prominent, opt-in, properly documented and easily withdrawn. If not, alter your consent mechanisms and seek fresh GDPR-compliant consent, or find an alternative to consent.

CHILDREN

You should start thinking now about whether you need to put systems in place to verify individuals' ages and to obtain parental or guardian consent for any data processing activity.

For the first time, the GDPR will bring in special protection for children's personal data, particularly in the context of commercial internet services such as social networking. If your organisation offers online services ('information society services') to children and relies on consent to collect information about them, then you may need a parent or guardian's consent in order to process their personal data lawfully. The GDPR sets the age when a child can give their own consent to this processing at 16 (although this may be lowered to a minimum of 13 in the UK). If a child is younger then you will need to get consent from a person holding 'parental responsibility'.

This could have significant implications if your organisation offers online services to children and collects their personal data. Remember that consent has to be verifiable and that when collecting children's data your privacy notice must be written in language that children will understand.

DATA BREACHES

You should make sure you have the right procedures in place to detect, report and investigate a personal data breach.

Some organisations are already required to notify the ICO (and possibly some other bodies) when they suffer a personal data breach. The GDPR introduces a duty on all organisations to report certain types of data breach to the ICO, and in some cases, to individuals. You only have to notify the ICO of a breach where it is likely to result in a risk to the rights and freedoms of individuals – if, for example, it could result in discrimination, damage to reputation, financial loss, loss of confidentiality or any other significant economic or social disadvantage.

Where a breach is likely to result in a high risk to the rights and freedoms of individuals, you will also have to notify those concerned directly in most cases.

You should put procedures in place to effectively detect, report and investigate a personal data breach. You may wish to assess the types of personal data you hold and document where you would be required to notify the ICO or affected individuals if a breach occurred. Larger organisations will need to develop policies and procedures for managing data breaches. Failure to report a breach when required to do so could result in a fine, as well as a fine for the breach itself.

It has always been good practice to adopt a privacy by design approach and to carry out a Privacy Impact Assessment (PIA) as part of this.

However, the GDPR makes privacy by design an express legal requirement, under the term 'data protection by design and by default'. It also makes PIAs – referred to as 'Data Protection Impact Assessments' or DPIAs – mandatory in certain circumstances.

A DPIA is required in situations where data processing is likely to result in high risk to individuals, for example:

•   where a new technology is being deployed;

•   where a profiling operation is likely to significantly affect individuals; or

•   where there is processing on a large scale of the special categories of data.

If a DPIA indicates that the data processing is high risk, and you cannot sufficiently address those risks, you will be required to consult the ICO to seek its opinion as to whether the processing operation complies with the GDPR.

You should therefore start to assess the situations where it will be necessary to conduct a DPIA. Who will do it? Who else needs to be involved? Will the process be run centrally or locally?

You should also familiarise yourself now with the guidance the ICO has produced on PIAs as well as guidance from the Article 29 Working Party, and work out how to implement them in your organisation. This guidance shows how PIAs can link to other organisational processes such as risk management and project management.

DATA PROTECTION OFFICERS

You should designate someone to take responsibility for data protection compliance and assess where this role will sit within your organisation's structure and governance arrangements.

You should consider whether you are required to formally designate a Data Protection Officer (DPO). You must designate a DPO if you are:

- a public authority (except for courts acting in their judicial capacity);

- an organisation that carries out the regular and systematic monitoring of individuals on a large scale; or

- an organisation that carries out the large scale processing of special categories of data, such as health records, or information about criminal convictions. The Article 29 Working Party has produced guidance for organisations on the designation, position and tasks of DPOs.

It is most important that someone in your organisation, or an external data protection advisor, takes proper responsibility for your data protection compliance and has the knowledge, support and authority to carry out their role effectively.

INTERNATIONAL

If your organisation operates in more than one EU member state, you should determine your lead data protection supervisory authority and document this.

The lead authority is the supervisory authority in the state where your main establishment is. Your main establishment is the location where your central administration in the EU is or else the location where decisions about the purposes and means of processing are taken and implemented.

This is only relevant where you carry out cross-border processing – ie you have establishments in more than one EU member state or you have a single establishment in the EU that carries out processing which substantially affects individuals in other EU states.

If this applies to your organisation, you should map out where your organisation makes its most significant decisions about its processing activities. This will help to determine your 'main establishment' and therefore your lead supervisory authority.

The Article 29 Working party has produced guidance on identifying a controller or processor's lead supervisory authority.

APPENDIX B

DATA PROTECTION POLICY FOR EMPLOYEES, WORKERS AND CONSULTANTS

© 2018 Employment Law Services Limited

IMPORTANT NOTICE

This policy does not constitute legal advice. The policy should be tailored to reflect the Employer's specific requirements following a data audit in accordance with the legislation, guidance and Codes of Practice issued by the Information Commissioner. This policy is designed to be used in conjunction with a Data Retention Policy and a Data Security Policy, which will be standard across your organisation and not specific to HR. It is recommended that specific legal advice is taken to ensure your compliance.

This policy assumes that you do not send data outside the EU or engage in automation/profiling.

Any liability for negligence or error, or any losses caused by reliance on this policy, is limited to the price paid to Employment Law Services Limited for this policy or £100, whichever is the greater.

DATA PROTECTION POLICY FOR EMPLOYEES, WORKERS AND CONSULTANTS

1 OVERVIEW

1.1 The Company takes the security and privacy of your data seriously. We need to gather and use information or 'data' about you as part of our business and to manage our relationship with you. We intend to comply with our legal obligations under the Data Protection Act 2018 (the '2018 Act') and the EU General Data Protection Regulation ('GDPR') in respect of data privacy and security. We have a duty to notify you of the information contained in this policy.

1.2 This policy applies to current and former employees, workers, volunteers, apprentices and consultants. If you fall into one of these categories then you are a 'data subject' for the purposes of this policy. You should read this policy alongside your contract of employment (or contract for services) and any other notice we issue to you from time to time in relation to your data.

1.3 [The Company has separate policies and privacy notices in place in respect of job applicants, customers, suppliers and other categories of data subject. A copy of these can be obtained from [insert].]

1.4   The Company has measures in place to protect the security of your data in accordance with our Data Security Policy. A copy of this can be obtained from [insert name].

1.5   The company will hold data in accordance with our Data Retention Policy. A copy of this can be obtained from [insert name]. We will only hold data for as long as necessary for the purposes for which we collected it.

1.6   The Company is a 'data controller' for the purposes of your personal data. This means that we determine the purpose and means of the processing of your personal data.

1.7   This policy explains how the Company will hold and process your information. It explains your rights as a data subject. It also explains your obligations when obtaining, handling, processing or storing personal data in the course of working for, or on behalf of, the Company.

1.8   This policy does not form part of your contract of employment (or contract for services if relevant) and can be amended by the Company at any time. It is intended that this policy is fully compliant with the 2018 Act and the GDPR. If any conflict arises between those laws and this policy, the Company intends to comply with the 2018 Act and the GDPR.

2 DATA PROTECTION PRINCIPLES

2.1   Personal data must be processed in accordance with six 'Data Protection Principles.' It must:

- be processed fairly, lawfully and transparently;

- be collected and processed only for specified, explicit and legitimate purposes;

- be adequate, relevant and limited to what is necessary for the purposes for which it is processed;

- be accurate and kept up to date. Any inaccurate data must be deleted or rectified without delay;

- not be kept for longer than is necessary for the purposes for which it is processed; and

- be processed securely.

We are accountable for these principles and must be able to show that we are compliant.

3 HOW WE DEFINE PERSONAL DATA

3.1   'Personal data' means information which relates to a living person who can be identified from that data (a 'data subject') on its own, or when taken together with other information which is likely to come into our possession. It includes any expression of opinion about the person and an indication of the intentions of us or others, in respect of that person. It does not include anonymised data.

3.2   This policy applies to all personal data whether it is stored electronically, on paper or on other materials.

3.3   This personal data might be provided to us by you, or someone else (such as a former employer, your doctor, or a credit reference agency), or it could be created by us. It could be provided or created during the recruitment process or during the course of the contract of employment (or services) or after its termination. It could be created by your manager or other colleagues.

3.4   We will collect and use the following types of personal data about you:

*   recruitment information such as your application form and CV, references, qualifications and membership of any professional bodies and details of any pre-employment assessments;

*   your contact details and date of birth;

*   the contact details for your emergency contacts;

*   your gender;

*   your marital status and family details;

*   information about your contract of employment (or services) including start and end dates of employment, role and location, working hours, details of promotion, salary (including details of previous remuneration), pension, benefits and holiday entitlement;

*   your bank details and information in relation to your tax status including your national insurance number;

*   your identification documents including passport and driving licence and information in relation to your immigration status and right to work for us;

- information relating to disciplinary or grievance investigations and proceedings involving you (whether or not you were the main subject of those proceedings);

- information relating to your performance and behaviour at work;

- training records;

- electronic information in relation to your use of IT systems/swipe cards/telephone systems;

- your images (whether captured on CCTV, by photograph or video);

- [ADD ANY OTHER TYPES OF PERSONAL DATA WHICH YOU HOLD FOR EMPLOYEES/WORKERS/CONSULTANTS]; and

- any other category of personal data which we may notify you of from time to time.

4   HOW WE DEFINE SPECIAL CATEGORIES OF PERSONAL DATA

4.1   'Special categories of personal data' are types of personal data consisting of information as to:

- your racial or ethnic origin;

- your political opinions;

- your religious or philosophical beliefs;

- your trade union membership;

- your genetic or biometric data;

- your health;

- your sex life and sexual orientation; and

- any criminal convictions and offences.

We may hold and use any of these special categories of your personal data in accordance with the law.

5 HOW WE DEFINE PROCESSING

5.1 'Processing' means any operation which is performed on personal data such as:

- collection, recording, organisation, structuring or storage;

- adaption or alteration;

- retrieval, consultation or use;

- disclosure by transmission, dissemination or otherwise making available;

- alignment or combination; and

- restriction, destruction or erasure.

This includes processing personal data which forms part of a filing system and any automated processing.

6 HOW WILL WE PROCESS YOUR PERSONAL DATA?

6.1 The Company will process your personal data (including special categories of personal data) in accordance with our obligations under the 2018 Act.

6.2 We will use your personal data for:

- performing the contract of employment (or services) between us;

- complying with any legal obligation; or

- if it is necessary for our legitimate interests (or for the legitimate interests of someone else). However, we can only do this if your interests and rights do not override ours (or theirs). You have the right to challenge our legitimate interests and request that we stop this processing. See details of your rights in section 12 below.

We can process your personal data for these purposes without your knowledge or consent. We will not use your personal data for an unrelated purpose without telling you about it and the legal basis that we intend to rely on for processing it.

If you choose not to provide us with certain personal data you should be aware that we may not be able to carry out certain parts of the contract between us. For example, if you do not provide us with your bank account details we may not be able to pay you. It might also stop us from complying with certain legal obligations and duties which we have such as to pay the right amount of tax to HMRC or to make reasonable adjustments in relation to any disability you may suffer from.

7   EXAMPLES OF WHEN WE MIGHT PROCESS YOUR PERSONAL DATA

7.1   We have to process your personal data in various situations during your recruitment, employment (or engagement) and even following termination of your employment (or engagement).

7.2   For example (and see section 7.6 below for the meaning of the asterisks):

- to decide whether to employ (or engage) you;

- to decide how much to pay you, and the other terms of your contract with us;

- to check you have the legal right to work for us;

- to carry out the contract between us including where relevant, its termination;

- training you and reviewing your performance*;

- to decide whether to promote you;

- to decide whether and how to manage your performance, absence or conduct*;

- to carry out a disciplinary or grievance investigation or procedure in relation to you or someone else;

- to determine whether we need to make reasonable adjustments to your workplace or role because of your disability*;

- to monitor diversity and equal opportunities*;

- to monitor and protect the security (including network security) of the Company, of you, our other staff, customers and others;

- to monitor and protect the health and safety of you, our other staff, customers and third parties*;

- to pay you and provide pension and other benefits in accordance with the contract between us*;

- paying tax and national insurance;

- to provide a reference upon request from another employer;

- to pay trade union subscriptions*;

- monitoring compliance by you, us and others with our policies and our contractual obligations*;

- to comply with employment law, immigration law, health and safety law, tax law and other laws which affect us*;

- to answer questions from insurers in respect of any insurance policies which relate to you*;

- running our business and planning for the future;

- the prevention and detection of fraud or other criminal offences;

- to defend the Company in respect of any investigation or

litigation and to comply with any court or tribunal orders for disclosure*;

- [INSERT ANY OTHER TIMES WHEN YOU MAY PROCESS PERSONAL DATA]; and

- for any other reason which we may notify you of from time to time.

7.3   We will only process special categories of your personal data (see above) in certain situations in accordance with the law. For example, we can do so if we have your explicit consent. If we asked for your consent to process a special category of personal data then we would explain the reasons for our request. You do not need to consent and can withdraw consent later if you choose by contacting [insert].

7.4   We do not need your consent to process special categories of your personal data when we are processing it for the following purposes, which we may do:

- where it is necessary for carrying out rights and obligations under employment law;

- where it is necessary to protect your vital interests or those of another person where you/they are physically or legally incapable of giving consent;

- where you have made the data public;

- where processing is necessary for the establishment, exercise or defence of legal claims; and

- where processing is necessary for the purposes of occupational medicine or for the assessment of your working capacity.

- [PUBLIC SECTOR EMPLOYERS MAY WISH TO ADD ADDITIONAL RELEVANT CATEGORIES CONTAINED IN CLAUSE 9 OF 2018 ACT]

7.5   [IF EMPLOYER INTENDS TO PROCESS INFORMATION ABOUT CRIMINAL CONVICTIONS THIS SHOULD BE EXPLAINED, ALONG WITH THE REASONS FOR IT IN ACCORDANCE.]

7.6   We might process special categories of your personal data for the purposes in paragraph 7.2 above which have an asterisk beside them. In particular, we will use information in relation to:

- your race, ethnic origin, religion, sexual orientation or gender to monitor equal opportunities;

- your sickness absence, health and medical conditions to monitor your absence, assess your fitness for work, to pay you benefits, to comply with our legal obligations under employment law including to make reasonable adjustments and to look after your health and safety; and

- your trade union membership to pay any subscriptions and to comply with our legal obligations in respect of trade union members.

- [EMPLOYER TO ADD ANY OTHER REASONS FOR PROCESSING SPECIAL CATEGORIES OF PERSONAL DATA]

7.7   We do not take automated decisions about you using your personal data or use profiling in relation to you. [IF AUTOMATION/ PROFILING IS USED THEN EXPLAIN]

8   SHARING YOUR PERSONAL DATA

8.1   Sometimes we might share your personal data with group companies or our contractors and agents to carry out our obligations under our contract with you or for our legitimate interests. [EMPLOYER TO ADD OTHER SITUATIONS]

8.2   We require those companies to keep your personal data confidential and secure and to protect it in accordance with the law and our policies. They are only permitted to process your data for the lawful purpose for which it has been shared and in accordance with our instructions.

8.3   [EMPLOYER TO SET OUT THE LEGITIMATE ACTIVITIES WHICH THIRD PARTIES DO, SUCH AS PAYROLL.]

8.4   We do not send your personal data outside the European Economic Area. If this changes you will be notified of this and the protections which are in place to protect the security of your data will be explained. [EMPLOYER TO CONFIRM WHETHER DATA WILL BE SENT OUTSIDE THE EU AND IF SO, WHAT PROTECTIONS ARE IN PLACE.]

9   HOW SHOULD YOU PROCESS PERSONAL DATA FOR THE COMPANY?

9.1   Everyone who works for, or on behalf of, the Company has some responsibility for ensuring data is collected, stored and handled appropriately, in line with this policy and the Company's Data Security and Data Retention policies.

9.2   The Company's Data Protection Officer/Data Protection Manager [insert details] is responsible for reviewing this policy and updating the Board of Directors on the Company's data protection responsibilities and any risks in relation to the processing of data. You should direct any questions in relation to this policy or data protection to this person.

9.3   You should only access personal data covered by this policy if you need it for the work you do for, or on behalf of the Company and only if you are authorised to do so. You should only use the data for the specified lawful purpose for which it was obtained.

9.4   You should not share personal data informally.

9.5   You should keep personal data secure and not share it with unauthorised people.

9.6   You should regularly review and update personal data which you have to deal with for work. This includes telling us if your own contact details change.

9.7   You should not make unnecessary copies of personal data and should keep and dispose of any copies securely.

9.8   You should use strong passwords.

9.9   You should lock your computer screens when not at your desk.

9.10   [Personal data should be encrypted before being transferred electronically to authorised external contacts. [Speak to IT for more information on how to do this.]]

9.11   Consider anonymising data or using separate keys/codes so that the data subject cannot be identified.

9.12   Do not save personal data to your own personal computers or other devices.

9.13   Personal data should never be transferred outside the European Economic Area except in compliance with the law and authorisation of the Data Protection Officer [insert name].

9.14   You should lock drawers and filing cabinets. Do not leave paper with personal data lying about.

9.15   You should not take personal data away from Company's premises without authorisation from your line manager or Data Protection Officer.

9.16   Personal data should be shredded and disposed of securely when you have finished with it.

9.17   You should ask for help from our Data Protection Officer/Data Protection Manager if you are unsure about data protection or if you notice any areas of data protection or security we can improve upon.

9.18   Any deliberate or negligent breach of this policy by you may result in disciplinary action being taken against you in accordance with our disciplinary procedure.

9.19   It is a criminal offence to conceal or destroy personal data which is part of a subject access request (see below). This conduct would also amount to gross misconduct under our disciplinary procedure, which could result in your dismissal.

9.20   [EMPLOYER TO ADD ANY OTHER RULES]

10   HOW TO DEAL WITH DATA BREACHES

10.1   We have robust measures in place to minimise and prevent data breaches from taking place. Should a breach of personal data occur (whether in respect of you or someone else) then we must take notes and keep evidence of that breach. If the breach is likely to result in a risk to the rights and freedoms of individuals then we must also notify the Information Commissioner's Office within 72 hours.

10.2   If you are aware of a data breach you must contact [insert name] immediately and keep any evidence you have in relation to the breach.

11   SUBJECT ACCESS REQUESTS

11.1   Data subjects can make a 'subject access request' ('SAR') to find out the information we hold about them. This request must be made in writing. If you receive such a request you should forward it immediately to the Data Protection Officer/Data Protection Manager who will coordinate a response.

11.2   If you would like to make a SAR in relation to your own personal data you should make this in writing to [insert name]. We must respond within one month unless the request is complex or numerous in which case the period in which we must respond can be extended by a further two months.

11.3   There is no fee for making a SAR. However, if your request is manifestly unfounded or excessive we may charge a reasonable administrative fee or refuse to respond to your request.

12 YOUR DATA SUBJECT RIGHTS

12.1   You have the right to information about what personal data we process, how and on what basis as set out in this policy.

12.2   You have the right to access your own personal data by way of a subject access request (see above).

12.3   You can correct any inaccuracies in your personal data. To do you should contact [insert name].

12.4   You have the right to request that we erase your personal data where we were not entitled under the law to process it or it is no longer necessary to process it for the purpose it was collected. To do so you should contact [insert name].

12.5   While you are requesting that your personal data is corrected or erased or are contesting the lawfulness of our processing, you can apply for its use to be restricted while the application is made. To do so you should contact [insert name].

12.6   You have the right to object to data processing where we are relying on a legitimate interest to do so and you think that your rights and interests outweigh our own and you wish us to stop.

12.7   You have the right to object if we process your personal data for the purposes of direct marketing.

12.8   You have the right to receive a copy of your personal data and to transfer your personal data to another data controller. We will not charge for this and will in most cases aim to do this within one month.

12.9 With some exceptions, you have the right not to be subjected to automated decision-making.

12.10 You have the right to be notified of a data security breach concerning your personal data.

12.11 In most situations we will not rely on your consent as a lawful ground to process your data. If we do however request your consent to the processing of your personal data for a specific purpose, you have the right not to consent or to withdraw your consent later. To withdraw your consent, you should contact [insert name].

12.12 You have the right to complain to the Information Commissioner. You can do this be contacting the Information Commissioner's Office directly. Full contact details including a helpline number can be found on the Information Commissioner's Office website (www.ico.org.uk). This website has further information on your rights and our obligations.

OTHER BOOKS BY DANIEL BARNETT

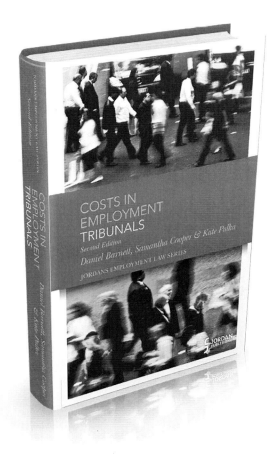

COSTS IN
EMPLOYMENT
TRIBUNALS

Second Edition

Daniel Barnett, Samantha Cooper & Kate Palka

JORDANS EMPLOYMENT LAW SERIES

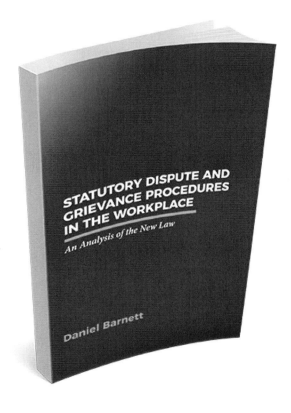

STATUTORY DISPUTE AND
GRIEVANCE PROCEDURES
IN THE WORKPLACE
An Analysis of the New Law

Daniel Barnett

HOW TO
**BOOST YOUR
PROFITS**
IN A
RECESSION

**INTELLIGENT
MARKETING for
EMPLOYMENT
LAWYERS**

by DANIEL BARNETT and EUGENIE VERNEY

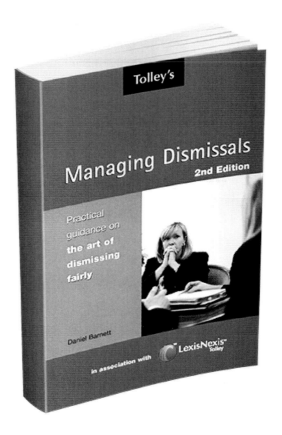

Tolley's

Managing Dismissals
2nd Edition

Practical guidance on the art of dismissing fairly

Daniel Barnett

in association with LexisNexis Tolley

AGE
Discrimination
An analysis of the
Employment Equality
(Age) Regulations 2006

by
Daniel
BARNETT
&
Kate
PALKA

IN SEARCHABLE PDF FORMAT

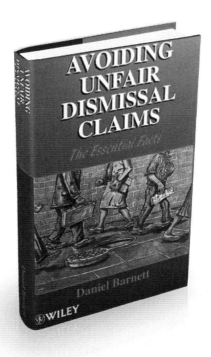

ONE FINAL THING...

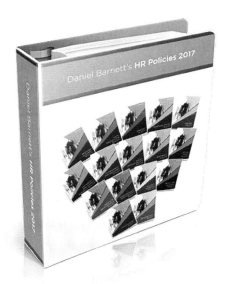

As a thank you for buying this book on GDPR for HR Professionals, I'd like to offer you a 50% discount on my 16 Employment Law Policies for small businesses.

If you are an HR professional, they are perfect for incorporating into a staff handbook. If you are a solicitor, they come with a licence for you to resell them or give them away for free to clients.